My Hibiscus
in the Sunrise

by Krystalann Bies

RoseDog Books
PITTSBURGH, PENNSYLVANIA 15238

RoseDog Books
585 Alpha Drive
Suite 103
Pittsburgh, PA 15238
Visit our website at *www.rosedogbookstore.com*

ISBN: 979-8-88812-400-0
eISBN: 979-8-88812-900-5

To the women who have made my soul roar like a lion.

Table of Contents

Dear Reader

Would you come with me on this journey to learn the complexities of female relationships? The good, the bad, the ugly? I'll be with you until the final chapter.

Love,
Your Writer.

Part 1:
The beginning: hymns of hope.

My Iris

Our bond began before I was even born, you knew about my existence before I even heard your voice. I had an unhealthy obsession with you. The kind that would make me write your name on things, blow up your phone with text messages, or bring you up in any conversation I had the opportunity to. What is it about you?

When we lock eyes, I'm torn between wanting to dance with you or wanting to numb the pain. I think it's a game that doesn't need to be played, but I'm used to giving myself unnecessary pain. And, then there's the game of touch. I don't know why when a single touch happens electricity and water begin to mix. It's never a combo that even I would come up with, but with you, knowing you, it makes sense in the most messed up way. The times I hated most were the moments when I tried to be gentle, and your body would either shake or you'd move as if I was this evil giant that was out to do malicious things to you. I wish you knew that I just wanted to be close to you, feel your warmth, receive your undivided attention, and to be your favorite person on this planet, or at least one of your favorites. I wanted you to love me as much as my mom does, something you will never have the capability of doing.

When the choice came down to either spending time with you or someone else, I'd always pick you. The decision always left never-ending butterflies in my stomach. I'd need dancing parties before being able to spend time with you. The dancing parties were needed if I were to allow the anxiety to escape my body.

I don't know how to share what we've grown to be without getting teary eyed. Your very presence has the ability to send shockwaves in my nervous system.

One minute I was good for you, because I was acting shy and quiet. You liked me better when I was controlled. Why didn't you give me attention when I would have moments of being hyper, loud, or obnoxious? Was I not as lovable then? Truth be told, I was a loud child, and somehow you always got to see my shy & masked side. Could you tell I was hiding a lot? Was my mask ever obvious to you?

I found that I couldn't run to you when I was bawling my eyes out. It was like you'd question my reasoning for crying so hard, then I'd have to force myself to stop the tears. I found that if I had something private to share I'd risk you sharing it with others or you having a blank expression. I wanted to trust, but as I grew in wisdom, I realized that if I wanted to fight for my own health, I'd have to pick my own battles. I needed to pick the people who wanted to support me, uplift me, didn't gossip, and didn't constantly make me feel like I was the one who was in the wrong. I didn't want to be with you if it meant my being with you derailed the healing. If it meant that I was being held to some impossible standard. If it meant that I had to question whether or not my hands were poison.

I wonder sometimes if my mom knew or could comprehend the impact or tiny bit of obsession I had of you when I was a teenager. I knew she knew I acted differently around you and for so long she wondered why. I know, at times, she would see the way you acted around or loved on me. She'd see how tight you'd hug me, she saw the moment everything shifted. Mom's know things.

I think one of my favorite moments was when I was 12 and we had just gotten ice cream. We locked eyes, and your smile grew and grew. It was then that I knew you were looking at me as if you were so proud of me. I hadn't done anything, yet there you were content, beautiful, and staring at me a little longer than usual. I felt warmness in my cheeks, unable to formulate or contain any emotions. I was wearing them all, all at once. I felt naked, but then, as life has it, people tend to chime in at the most inappropriate of times. I quickly smiled at you while attending to other people's inquiries, but I could see your gaze on me ever so often, not seeming bothered at all. I liked seeing you in the corner of my eye.

I'd love sitting on your lap, with you pulling me in. I'd catch a smell of laundry detergent and that's how I knew it was you, and not anybody else. You're the only one who smelled fresh, clean, and like you just landed straight out of the dryer. I was drawn to the smell, you see, because I think I had become accustomed to the smell of smoke at my own home. Yet, my sense of smell and lungs never waivered.

You taught me the importance of praying, but more importantly praying for others. I learned how to pray out loud and proudly from you. I learned the right way of setting the table, to invite the people in the corner, and to see beauty & fun in having absolutely no plans in a day.

I think what breaks me is that you've grown accustomed to a marriage where the other person doesn't know the depth or meaning of your relationship with Jesus. We've had very intimate moments together in prayer, and even in my own young age, I could see your relationship with the Savior was much deeper than most people close in my life. That always fascinated me, made me hungry for whatever you had. Shouldn't that make your spouse gallop in the field after you? I know things that maybe I shouldn't, that doesn't mean I want you to wallow in sorrow.

I want you to chase the sun, your dreams, to be deeply loved by the good, bad, and ugly.

You are worthy, deserving of a second chance at life. Because our upbringings were similar I can resonate with your pain and the idea to numb the uncomfortable.

My question is: do you think about me everyday as much as I think about you?

I don't even think I can comprehend how much I love you or why your impact is still so instrumental to me today. I can't count how many times I've been on my knees wondering about such things.

I know you sometimes see me, perhaps hear me. I know that we both know whatever happens thy will be done. And, isn't that enough?

My First Dream

Shortly after I was first abused, you were introduced. I encountered the same dream, what seemed to be everyday to now once a year, where you appeared and preyed on my young mind.

The dream starts and I always instantly feel paralyzed, unable to catch a breath. I'd see you in the store with light hair and large hips. Your hands kept finding ways to your hips, you'd smile, and then gaze deeply into my soul. Even my 5 year old self could pick up on your perverted games by your uncomfortably long stare. It felt sexual, it felt dangerous, and there had to be a way out. Then you'd get up to come near me, to find my hands, to do what? My eyes would close and the dream would always stop there.

What could happen after that?

Are you real? Are you out there? Do you, too, have the same disgusting dream every year?

I can't inherently remember you touching my tiny self, but if you're real, I can say that I'll always remember how the room felt, and that rattles me.

My First Friend

My gosh you always smelled like scented candles. But, my goodness did we have similar traumas going on. Last time I saw you we were both 8.

You were a friend from childhood and it still somewhat irks me that I know that our parents weren't friends. Our parents, I feel, would have been good for one another. Yet, when I think about our friendship I know we weren't good for each other. I succumbed to the life I felt I deserved when I was around you. Of course there was some normalcy to our friendship. We would spend hours on the swings or playing in our jeeps. But, somehow we would find ourselves back in your room playing house. I think at one point it got old what we were doing, and it felt wrong, just like with that boy. It never felt fulfilling and it's not supposed to at that age.

You were neighbors with the boy who ripped my youth, and in that we played a similar game. Same gender, same age, same messed up minds, but deeply loved by a king. It wasn't good that we spent time alone. When I was being abused by that boy, that same confusion and numbing was being brought to our time together.

The weird thing about the street you lived on was another girl that was neighbors with you was also abusing me at the same time. What was it about that street that screamed prey on children, brainwash them into thinking that was all they were worthy of, and leave them with forever questions?

I wonder about you from time to time. Are you a mom now? Are you married? Are you happy? Are you living with the nightmares of your own trauma? Do you have faith?

All these questions may never be answered, but one thing will always remain: with all the healing I have gotten, I know your story is not done, and with complete confidence I can say I love you.

The Other Mom

66Mom, she's got eggplants!" (I meant implants). That's my earliest memory of you, which I know sounds oddly inappropriate, but I wasn't taught clear boundaries. I told my mom about your large boobs, because I felt when you hugged me, it was right in my face. You didn't abuse me or make me feel unloved, but that is my earliest memory of you.

You would always make the best food, help me with my hair, cuddle with me, and give me the warmest of hugs. Your hugs had the ability to make me feel seen, safe, and loved, something I always had craved with my own mother. I had an obsession with your hugs, with your loving touch, with your beauty. I wasn't confused by the love you had for me, because it was clear from the beginning I was deeply loved by you.

What was confusing to me was once I moved away the gap in time when I would see you. I was heartbroken, confused, overwhelmed with my own big feelings, and questioned myself. I wondered if you were mad at me, if there was something wrong with me, or if you were just done with me like some adults were.

One day, when I was 16, you said that it would stop being less inconsistent of seeing me. I hung onto your words as if I was holding onto the steering wheel of a car on a slippery road. It was risky to hold onto your words, because seeing you did become so inconsistent. I just wanted a consistent parent in my life, some stability or a schedule of when I could see you. I didn't think that was too much.

I began the journey of seeing you yearly at either Thanksgiving or Christmas, and I selfishly tried holding onto you tighter than ever before. I wanted you to see that I was worthy of your time, that you had enough room in your heart for me, that I had changed and became more mature. As with my dad, you weren't impressed with my behavior, how I would speak or treat others. You were convinced with your own assumptions, not once checking in to see how this all made me feel.

I wish I didn't hold onto you so tight, because I needed to cling to the promise of Jesus. People are going to disappoint you, but Jesus never will.

I think of you everyday, sometimes obsessing over what I could have done differently. I'm grateful you came to all of my ceremonies whether it be from high school or college. I'm grateful you supported my earliest dream of dancing and acting. I am most grateful that you saw me as more than the sexual abuse I endured, that I was strong enough to keep pressing on. And, I'm honored and blessed for all the moments you held my hand whether crossing the street or when I was crying.

Your beauty can leave anyone to stop in their tracks. Even my own mother has always been in awe of your stunning self.

The seasons have changed, but one thing remains: my deep love and appreciation of you.

Dear Reader:

"All I want is to live within Your love, be undone by who You are
My desire is to know You deeper.
Lord, I will open up again
Throw my fears into the wind, I am desperate for a touch of heaven."
                                                    -Hillsong Worship.

May the worship music be healing to your bones.

                    Love,
                    Your Writer.

*I have wrestled and I have trembled toward surrender…" —
Hillsong United.*

My First Touch of Heaven

The first friend I let in, who saw the not so pretty parts of me, and showed me God's grace, I thank you.

Reflecting on one of the sweetest days of my life makes me think of the scene from Forest Gump and Forest gets on the bus, everyone just keeps rejecting him, except one angel who saw him beyond his disabilities.

One day in third grade it was a brutally cold day out, and I was out on the playground, just freezing. Then all of a sudden a girl appeared out of nowhere, and said in the most angelic voice ever, "Are you cold?" She not only shared some of her things with me, but she wrapped me up, and I felt as if I was being comforted by a mother. I was undone by the simple kindness, but I was convinced no one in this small town would ever like me, let alone love me. I was too messed up.

The blistering cold meant nothing to your warm heart. 3rd grade. You held me. You reminded me that good people still existed.

I'd like to think God knew what He was doing when we were placed in the same classroom in 4th grade. We'd sneak notes during class, and I'd always be giddy. We thought we were so sneaky, as if we were in our own world. We were so young, though. We had big ideas and we were both determined individuals, so we sought some plans to paper. Believe me, we were swooning over sheets of paper. Yes, paper. We dreamt up our families by magazines, we crafted our futures. The list was endless. We brought this with us into 5th grade.

By the time 5th grade came rolling around the corner, we had been to each other's houses, wrote those notes in class, and our parents had become friends by this point, but something was drastically different once we walked through those doors. We didn't have the same classroom, but our paths crossed more and more than the years prior. We had other friends and people to talk to, but as the months went on, we found ways to be creative about the ways in which we spent time together. Our friendship deepened. It wasn't until December of 2008 that I let some walls down. We would ride a bus together after school to transfer over to another school to switch busses, and it was often our time to listen to music and talk about our dreams. One particular day something shifted, like I said. I believe this was the day we really became best friends. I had been questioning why someone would be this kind to me. This girls heart had tripled since the first time I met her and I didn't think that would be possible, BUT IT DID. So, I nervously and bravely asked her, "Why are you so good to me?" In my head I thought I wasn't good enough to have a friend like this, I was so messed up and had so many issues. Then she said in the most angelic way, "Because I love you!" Then she grabbed me and hugged me. I never had a friend say or do something like that to me, so I fought the tears that wanted to escape, and settled with the feeling of relief. This was also the time you introduced me to Taylor Swift, because I had got an MP3 as a gift.

As time went on, my obsession with Taylor Swift music became so real, but so did the long conversations on the phone, the sleepovers, and everyday life. I'd listen to the music to force the tears out when things wouldn't go well in the friendship. We had small things that would come up, of course.

By spring, someone who abused me was in jail, and I'd been sexually abused twice between March 27 to April 9th. That was a lot and so confusing, but something that always distracted me was celebrations. My birthday party consumed my mind.

I invited so many people to my 5th grade birthday party, but I'd be lying if I said I really only wanted some alone time with you.

What we had was so beautiful and not even Taylor Swift lyrics could capture the friendship eloquently. You gave me the most beautiful card and

CD of all Taylor Swift songs. You kept making sure I felt special that day, and did I? I was over the moon.

On the last day of 5th grade we ran around the school taking pictures with my mom's professional camera, and dreamed up one last enchanted get-away on the playground. We said our goodbyes to this school, because we'd be in middle school in the fall.

~

God: You planted the seed, you always were faithful in the timing of the friendship, and how it was orchestrated. The seasons changed, the friendship changed. It withered away, but the love didn't.

~

After 6th grade we drifted more and more, becoming friends with other people and deepening those friendships, and expanding our hearts to different opportunities. Yet, our love for Jesus, music, and people somehow and someway kept our paths aligned in a way. We had choir together in middle school, and again in high school.

In high school you were the first person to tell me about a suicide, due to my lack of being on Facebook over the weekend. I was the first to introduce you to the movie The Last Song. You had been wanting to see it for a long while, and in 10th grade, I convinced you to come over to watch the movie with me. At this stage of our life, we were more mature, but when we were together, we couldn't help, but unleash our child-like wonder and hope. You always reminded me that good people still existed when we would spend time together.

That was the last time we spent alone time together. As the years passed and we prepared for graduation, a smile and appreciation for the other was never far. Even on our last day of high school we sat next together and snapped one last pic. We even invited each other to our graduation parties, though we both had other prior obligations those days.

Something must have happened from that last day, though. Something shattered, some type of division was created. An awkward interaction in 2019 made me question everything. Could I have possibly dreamed up this angelic human being? Do hearts change that much?

Whatever the case, the love remains, and the song continues on.

My First Mentor

When we first met I had severe issues, but you saw something unique in me. Looking back I can tell you had deep love and care for me, though in the moment I was convinced you could never love me. I moved to a small town where no one knew me, and I was carrying around a massive secret, that I was molested for a long time, and that it influenced everything I did. On paperwork you mentioned that I had problems with touching myself in class and it's shocking I didn't hate you after I read that. Yet, the deep love you had for me pumped through your veins the more time we spent together.

I still remember the first time I bought you a gift. I think I was hoping that would be a clear indication that you needed to love me. But, you already did and it was so obvious, perhaps even to an unborn child.

As the years passed our families even became close. One year, however, the enemy tried to separate us. You were switching titles and I wasn't going to see you everyday. My mom sat with you on the phone as she tried to fight tears in her eyes about what the next year would bring. I realized then the impact you had not just on me, but on my whole entire family.

The enemy didn't come close to winning that year. Somehow by the miraculous work of God our paths crossed more than we expected. And, on one unexpected afternoon you chose to do the grandest gesture. Thinking back on that day still moves me to my knees. You became a hero in my story that day and I don't even know if you know why. One day, while in school, you stopped by my school and tried tracking me down. You told teachers that you were looking for me and they notified me. I thought, "my gosh, she's looking for me? Why me?" I remember being overwhelmed by emotions and confused by my feelings about you. I was in 5th grade, just beginning the whole puberty process and everything was confusing. And, you were looking for me as if I was an important person in your life. Important person in your life? What? The person who had millions of friends??? I, being the naive and childish kid I was, chose to hide from you. I hid by the lockers when all of a sudden I hear footsteps coming down the hallway, and you spotted me right away. My hands were shaking and I was stunned to see you in the flesh. You had the biggest smile on your face and you didn't stop your fast pace of a walk until I was buried deep into your embrace. You held me there for a long while. I think I totally zoned out, because when you let me go I was unsure of where or how you got there. I was experiencing heaven and heaven always felt far away at my house. When you let go of me and you created a space for me to collect myself, you told me you had something for me. You took out a small bag of gifts for me that you had gotten on a trip with a card and said, "I thought about you." Looking back at the card it had to have said "I love you" a thousand times all over without actually putting the words on the paper. It was just that obvious, because that was the kind of person you were. I was undone and felt bashful, and you kept smiling at me with the "I'm so proud of you, let the world see you shine now!" That day and that moment, I wish I could go back and soak it up. I'm glad it's forever edged in my memories.

More years passed, more family gatherings, and more moments to grow closer. So much fun and love had happened between us. You were my favorite person, the best part of the small town, and somehow everything changed after 6 years of knowing each other.

Freshman year of high school was the beginning of something we both didn't anticipate. It was the year you moved from being my mentor to my coach, a title we were both anxious about.

I'll never forget the moment I had tennis practice and my mom wasn't able to pick me up, and you selflessly drove me home. I was 14 years old, still ever so giddy about you, and wondering how we got to this moment. You proved to be even more amazing when you parked right outside my house. You turned to me, looked at me in the eyes, and we shared our first mature & deep conversation with one another. It felt natural and I was able to see the not so good parts about you and come to know the things you struggled with. That was the moment that changed everything about our relationship I feel like. Before was childish and fragile, and then we were moving towards an adult relationship, and I wasn't sure I was ready for it, but my gosh was I grateful. You trusted me, that was everything to me.

We had several more moments like these that made me draw to you. I was always captivated by your storytelling. You had a way of bringing people in like an addicting perfume.

As the years passed and our relationship deepened, we saw less of each other. We were no longer in the same town and catching up was just that much more sweet. In 2017 you were a safety blanket that I didn't know I needed from you. A few more years go by, and you became electric all over again. You would check in with me as any good mentor/friend would. You got me excited for graduating with my bachelors. I had several doubts that I could even finish and you were right there, being all loving and maternal as you have been our whole relationship.

.

.

.

I'll never forget a few months later you texting me to let me know you'd take me out to celebrate me graduating. I was giddy, counting down the days until I could see you. When we met for dinner it felt as if we were in a movie with soft music playing and voices non-existent. It was blissful, perfect in every way. Then we went for a walk to talk about everything. Four hours of pure grace and devotion.

A few texts here and there to check in with me about my new job to a new city and then...

It didn't take long for you to fall off the face of the earth. Fourteen years and then not even a phone call or text to let me know what was going on in your heart. I would have sat, listened to your tender heart.

Though the seasons have changed, and the Lord was faithful to plant the seed, my love for you will remain. I hope the depth of our love for one another will one day bring us back to each other.

"Good hymns are an immense blessing to the church. They train people for heaven, where praise is one of the principal occupations."
—J.C. Ryle.

My Favorite Teacher

The woman who is lovely & a servant of good deeds, that's what I am reminded of when I see your presence.

In 5th grade you turned my world upside down. When everything was clamorous and confusing, you were the one who brought steadiness to me. You had a way of making everyone in class feel loved, while still maintaining a sense of professionalism. You made reading exceptionally fun, always reminding us to tap into our imagination. Everyday you greeted us outside the classroom with the biggest smile and warmest hug, a rarity these days. You paved the way for future teachers, and it's truly uncanny to know we were the last class you'd teach, because at the end of the year you were celebrating retirement.

Yes, you had something that washed over your face that showed you were older, but you also looked so youthful and ever so playful.

You changed my life that year. I'll never forget being so proud of myself for being able to pick you up off of the ground, showing you that I had enough muscles. You never needed proof of my potential, you always knew.

As time went on I was blessed to see you around town, eventually being able to be friends on Facebook. You kept tabs on me, always figuring out my next move. We would even have long conversations on the phone, and you'd listen to me tell stories.

You'd even sometimes frustrate me, which broke me, because just looking at you could make anyone burst into a big smile.

As I got older and pursued more college, it became harder to see you. You valued your time with your grandkids. But, somehow with our conversations on the phone you'd find a way to give me hope we would spend time with each other soon. I'd always hold onto that.

But, then the tables turned. We had the most amazing conversation about summer, travels, marriage, and life lessons. You ended the conversation by saying, "I'm so glad we could talk today, honey." The term honey always has an influence on me. I felt loved.

Then, when a few weeks went by, I thought I'd ask again about setting something up, even if it meant a half hour walk. I wanted it more than anything.

You told me that right now family was your focus and that it would be best not to.

I hated the message you sent me, because I had been waiting over 3 years to finally get together again, and only to be crushed again. It was too much to fathom. Something had to give, so with grace I decided to move on, putting more than just space between us.

You will always be my favorite teacher who taught me the importance of being a kid, reading, faith, and leaving room for imagination. Jesus was definitely ever so kind to me for granting me 15 years of deep love from you.

If I see you again, I'll smile, and probably give you the warmest of hugs. I know I'll need it, hopefully you will, too.

Part 2:
Praises of Adolescence

My Blurred Lines

I was in 6th grade when we met, not even 12 years old. My friends and class were drawn to your intriguing, young appearance. People were confused by your age.

I got to see you everyday and found you take interest in my troubled life. You had told not only me, but others if we were in any kind of trouble that we could call you. I didn't miss that beat.

When the chaos at home felt unbearable and scary, I decided to call you one evening. I explained the details of my situation, only to hear you say, "I said only call for emergencies." You crushed my heart that night, but my heart was big and I still saw good in you.

Over the period of five months we gave each other three long notes. In the last note I included a gift, because it was Christmas time and I wanted you to know a fraction of what you meant to me. You were beyond delighted and I couldn't believe how much I was going to miss you over break.

You always showed up for me in the mornings with tight hugs, even if I purposely tried to walk by without getting one. I didn't want you to know that I was obsessed with receiving your embraces.

But, as time went on things weren't as clear and beautiful. You became confusing to me, unwilling to share what was going on in your complicated head of yours. Then for some reason, I was shamed by not knowing one of your boundaries.

In fact, when I showed up to school, in the summer, for activities, I was called into the guidance office, because you wanted to make sure there wasn't going to be uncomfortable or hard feelings. You made me feel as a young child that I wasn't good enough for a second chance and that whatever I may have done was going to be held over me for any time I would see you.

It's been 14 years now, and when we see each other, you still look at me the way you did the day everything ended.

I wish when I was young, innocent, and didn't know about boundaries, that you would have taught me one. Because, it would have saved so many years of mistrust of older adults.

I still love you, so I'm glad that you got what you wanted after so many years: two kids, happy marriage, and a loving home. I'm happy for you, but I can't help and wonder if you ever did that to some other child. Because, how could you look a child in the eyes and tell them they weren't worthy enough after one misunderstanding?

My Unreliable One

The thing about abusers, they can brainwash you, program your brain into thinking you want what they have to offer. I didn't want to be naked with you, I didn't want you to know me in that intimate kind of way. I didn't want you to know every scar, mole, or mark on my body.

Each time we got together, you'd learn a new art piece of my body, willing yourself there. We never went as far as having sex, but I mean what is sex between the same gender? What does that look like when you're 11? I wasn't fully developed, I didn't have my period, there was so much child still in me. I didn't understand why you wanted my body. I felt filthy and ruined. I received that feeling after first being molested at 5.

In a cave, I'd like to call it, where it was dark was where we did our best work. That was what I kept telling myself, because you couldn't see every mark that was scraped by a man. The scars felt visible to me, but they were only emotional ones, that left me damaged for years. Sometimes it felt aggressive, sometimes it felt like the longest gosh darn marathon of my life.

We'd stop once I hit a tingling sensation down there, and that's when I'd open my eyes realizing this wasn't just a dream, it was a continued nightmare. The game had to keep going on, because I was becoming good at it, I might even like it, and there was no escaping this prison any time soon, so I best become gosh darn used to it. Thankfully you never made me go down on you, but there was other things that felt could be just as gross as that.

When the last time did come, and routine became about routine, I wasn't conscious of what we were doing, just a robot obeying a game I was brainwashed into liking.

It did stop, but it took until my early 20s to come to terms that 1. I hated it. 2. It wasn't my fault.

Hearing your name come up in conversations still makes me squeal, sometimes raising goosebumps on my arms. Over the years I became okay with seeing you, sometimes at events, until I had healing and realized it wasn't okay to see you.

Today I can say I'm happy with how well you're doing in life, that you've received help and healing, but that doesn't mean I want to be in a room with you again anytime soon.

Dear Reader:

"If you're brave enough to leave behind everything familiar and comforting, which can be anything from your house to bitter old resentments, and set out on a truth-seeking journey, either externally or internally, and if you are truly willing to regard everything that happens to you on that journey as a clue and if you accept everyone you meet along the way as a teacher and if you are prepared, most of all, to face and forgive some very difficult realities about yourself, then the truth will not be withheld from you." -Elizabeth Gilbert.

Each person you meet, let them be as a teacher rather than a curse, because with each person you can learn something whether it was a good experience or bad one.

Love,
Your Writer

My Shy One

As with some of my friends, I don't know how we even began our path to each other. Other than I remember seeing you out of the corner of my eye, and thought you looked innocent, pure, shy, angelic, and so sweet.

You were only in 5th grade when we began our friendship and I was in 7th grade. We weren't even in the same school, yet I felt as if I saw you so often.

It amazes me still to this day, that during my most fake year of my life, I was the most real around you. I think it had to do with your angelic, lovely presence. You always had a way of making the room calm down, despite your often shy demeanor.

We would often meet at open gym on Sundays and talk for hours. You'd always smirk at me, wearing a pink-ish sweater, and had light brown hair that glistened in the sun.

We would have a few sleepovers. One time, right before we went to sleep, you confessed you feared you would lose me. You had tears in your eyes. I had never experienced anything like that before. I thought, "a friend is afraid to lose me? Why?" All I could do was grab you and hug you, unable to articulate what you said to me. It had a profound impact on me and I had no idea why.

When spring of 2010 came around I was hard-core planning my birthday party and I knew I needed you to be there. I knew you would be the youngest at my party, but if I wanted to stay true to my authentic self, I knew better to invite the young girl who would offer the reminder. We both had birthdays in

April, so it was a big month of celebration for us. I was, undoubtedly, looking forward to our time together.

I invited three girls to my birthday party. We all went to a Waterpark, filmed videos in the hotel room, and enjoyed hours of laughter. You never left my side, reminding me every moment to have fun, to let loose even.

I don't remember why we stopped being friends not long after my birthday party. Like most friends during that stage of my life, they grew tired of my excessive need for attention and affirmations. Your season in my life was cut short, but you always remained friendly to me, because by that fall we were finally in the same school as each other. I was in 8th grade, and you in 6th grade. I still protected you at times, but it was more at a distance, and somehow I managed to be okay with the distance.

We drifted. Your role, however, showed a lesson I took in future friendships.

You reminded me of God's certain characteristics: you were slow to anger and quick to listen and even quicker to show forgiveness. For that I'm forever grateful, because it led me to giving my heart to Jesus that summer.

"You can kiss your family and friends good-bye and put miles between you, but at the same time you carry them with you in your heart, your mind, your stomach, because you do not just live in a world but a world lives in you." —Frederick Buechner.

The People Pleaser

Meeting you in the fall of 2010 was humbling, wild, and intriguing. It often stirred my curiosity, for that I'm grateful, because I could tap into things learned and grow in wisdom.

Our relationship was often obsessive, consuming, and draining. I had never met someone who was addicted to their phone, to receiving and sending texts. When we would hang out alone, I'd have to compete between you and your phone, the phone always winning. I wanted your time, attention, to actually have a conversation, and you wanted to stay up to date with all your texts. I wondered what drove the obsession, but in time I was drawn to that world with you. I became enthralled into the world of technology, making sure I never missed a text from anyone, and often feeling incredibly guilty if I didn't get back to someone in a timely fashion. But, then I found myself getting upset with people who took hours to respond, a habit that followed me into adulthood. You'd have people reach out to me a few times, if I didn't respond to you right away, checking if I would respond to them. You'd eventually find out that I either got my phone taken away or I was attending to my family.

I think of the songs Teenage Dream and Back to December when I reflect back on our friendship, remembering how I'd always listen to them when things weren't going our way.

What I thought was the end of our friendship in the spring of 2011 turned to open a new door when you joined tennis my sophomore year and your freshman year. We had an extra two years of connection and fun in a sport we deeply loved. Our friendship became less obsessive and more mature, you finding a balance between your phone and in person conversations. When we first became friends you were in 7th grade and I was in 8th grade, and we were going through hormonal changes, drama, and the rollercoaster of emotions of being a teenager. Time and distance did help, but our relationship couldn't sustain once tennis ended. Too much drama came from our big friendship circle.

This friendship taught me many things, habits that took a long time to let go. People pleasing, obsessiveness, and phone addiction weren't things I was hoping to bring into adulthood.

Faith, healing, and time has allowed me to look back on our friendship with laughter, love, and tenderness. Maturity and love will do that, and that's beautiful.

My Scars

Do you remember our first hug? It feels like yesterday I was shopping with my mom at the store, and you were wearing that red jacket, wearing alien perfume, looking content and wonderful. You had the biggest smile, and fully embraced all that I was at that moment. Honestly you embraced all that I was every time we hugged and I was always undone by it.

You are a year younger than me, but always felt more wise and mature than I ever was. Yet, you'd convince me every time we were together to invite that inner child, to not only swing on the swings, but to get as close to the sky as possible, and then jump off. You were the most exciting thing about my middle school experience. You had an infectious personality, one that had everyone wrapped around your finger. Everyone swarmed your presence. I wondered if all the attention would get to your head. It only made you more of a humble, kind, and joyful human.

When you moved away I was devastated, unable to understand how such a sweet girl could move so far away.

That move destroyed you, people made you do things you swore you would never do, and people took advantage of you.

The amazing thing about our friendship is that even though God took you out of my life for seasons, we never went more than a year without sending some type of message to the other. I always knew I could check in with you, even if it was brief.

I don't miss waiting around for your texts, developing an unhealthy habit of growing attached to you, and being an overall terrible friend at the beginning. I am, however, grateful for the deep & passionate conversations we would have, the profound kind of love, the exhilarating feelings of our friendship, and the intimacy that was found within our long letters.

Our reunion will be as if we were never cutting friends, but broken friends that will need God's everlasting love.

To the friend who was there through texting when I first grabbed a knife to slash my wrists, and to the friend who was there the night I was trying to overdose on pills, you've seen my scariest moments.

My Scars, may we meet on the branches of a tree, hand in hand, ready to embark on any next adventure God may have for us. Because, the scars we both have can't compare to the love we have in our veins.

My Walls Down

The Lord was merciful, ever so particular about the timing of you landing on my path. You'll be marked on my heart forever for what you did for me as a teenager.

I met you in 2010 at Bible camp, shared my testimony with you, and in 2011 you became even more important to me. We only got the opportunity to spend time together three times before not seeing each for a decade. Sometimes it doesn't matter about how many times, but the amount of hours in those times that make a difference.

I expected you to be different after a decade of not seeing each other. But the phone conversations and texts didn't show me just how different. I was overwhelmed by the difference, the defensiveness, and protectiveness. You were no longer the laid back, chill, touchy, outgoing, and gentle human I had come to know you as. You were still kind, curious, generous, and showing people the hospitality spirit, though.

It's wild how so much of the world can consume someone instead of Jesus. When we focus our attention on the worldly desires, we forget our ultimate focus. I think what grabbed of your heart was of this world instead of what is in the Word.

You still pivoted my focus, rippled every broken trust that was taken for me, and showed me a trusted adult when I was 13 years old. That is something that can never be taken from me, that is something to Forever have a victory dance about.

That's my anthem, my hope, and cry that young children would find a trusted adult to unleash the darkest of secrets to. That it's okay to share what happened to you, that it makes you brave, not disgusting. That whatever happened can be a breath of a hallelujah instead of shame from the enemy.

What the enemy intended for evil, God can turn to good.

My Long Call

"Hi! Can we sit by you?" Those were the first words you said to me when we met at Acquire the Fire in January of 2011. It was a Christian event that had thousands of people falling deeply in love with Jesus.

We saw each other every Wednesday at youth group, but it wasn't until February that it went at lightning speed.

The week I self harmed for the first time, I hid that from you, even though a few days later I had a scheduled sleepover at your house. I went straight from my aunts house to yours and even though I wore sweaters, you somehow suspected that something was wrong. I felt like I was somehow with a detective, friend, and a mother. The combo didn't make any sense to me at the time, but it does now. I felt paranoid the first few hours that I was at your house, because I knew what I did was wrong, but it also felt wrong to keep such a secret hidden from you. Friends should be honest with each other and I couldn't bring myself to telling you something that was so shameful.

I don't remember how I told you, but I remember feeling safe, that I could trust you. I remember you saying, "I'm sad that you cut yourself." Well, it made me sad that you felt sad. You treated my cutting scandal into means of celebrating the plans God had for my future. We prayed, danced, took pictures, and took walks with your little sister. I truly had the best time. From that time on, I didn't hide anything from you. We spent long hours on the phone, often our parents having to tell us to get off, because we had other priorities to tend to.

When my birthday approached I had the same level of excitement as the year prior. This time I had about 15 girls joining my party to yet another water park. I can't remember much about it, other than minutes before we went to sleep. We had a disagreement about something, and you asked, looking me sternly in the eyes, "don't you know I love you?" I was lost for words, and then, unexpectedly, you came by my face to kiss my cheek. I never had a friend do that to me, but again you reminded me of a nurturing mother. You were 1.5 years older than me, and always showed depth and wisdom. Something you gifted me in a way.

We continued our fast paced friendship for about four or five months, until you know the worst day for me.

I'll never forget the last day of our friendship when your mom called my mom to share concerns about my emotional behavior. Your mom voiced that you felt it was a constant battle of going back and forth, not feeling good enough, and that it was time to take a break. I wish, now looking back, that you would have just taken the time to meet with me to tell how you were feeling. But, that's the past.

Now, 10 years later, you've walked away from religion, are helping raise your partners kids, and live with your partner. However, your love for nature, love for wisdom, and to see beauty in any person you meet still shines from you. I'm glad, because people need that. They need your sunshine, your taste in life.

Our chapter may have gotten cut too short, but then again, it was the perfect timing, because from you I needed to rise, and I have.

My Cuddle

In the fall of 2013 I encountered the movie, The Great Gatsby, in a new light because of you. You had the ability to rip the flaps of my heart wide open, and remind me to see every stitch of fabric, never missing a detail. You paid attention to details that people often skip over. You marveled at everything, you captivated hearts, and you invited physical touch back into my life.

When we became friends I was a junior, and you were a sophomore in high school. We were both broken from the year prior for different reasons, but in that pain, we found a way to each other that was often unhealthy. Everyday we snap chatted with each other. I often would forget tasks around the house, because I didn't want to miss out on a text from you.

At school we would find each other during breaks or lunch, often going to your house after school if I didn't have work, play practice, or tennis game/practice. It felt as if I had a single minute, I needed to be around you. I wanted to take care of you, be your friend, though I often tried to act as if I was your Savior. I'd run to your house and bring you care packages when you'd be sick or you'd go through a breakup, I was there. I'd sit with you in your bed, hold you close, and bask in gratefulness. I loved being in your presence, being safe, and content, because it was never that way at my own home.

The drama at school, our own separate home lives, and communication was always messy. Even though there were hilarious, fun, and sweet moments, it felt as if every other week we would try to end our friendship. We consumed so much of ourselves into the friendship, never giving the other space to breathe, to ever take a moment to shower in other friendships.

Our friendship couldn't sustain longer than a few months, but ever so often our hearts find each other, and we have nothing, but praise, love, and tenderness toward the other.

My France

The first I laid eyes on you, you were heading to the bathroom on crutches, and I held the door open for you. Your eyes were wide open with astonishment and thankfulness. You were convinced that the young had forgotten the simple, such as holding the door open for our elders. It was a natural thing for me to do.

By my junior year the kindness, fun, and generous personality rubbed off on many students. I'd hear about you in many conversations. You lived a mile away from me, your sons riding the bus with me, and yet, we still had not a real conversation.

It took some time, but each opportunity I had to visit your classroom during a free moment, I found ways to share something with you, something that both intrigued us.

You were a French teacher, so when the time came for you to go away with your students to Paris, I was devastated. We had built something, and then you were leaving. I was jealous and excited for all the students, though.

When you came back, I made sure to stop into your classroom first thing that morning. You had me close my eyes and gave me chocolate, and the most beautiful scarf. It was lime green with glitter all over it. It meant so much to me. It was then that I realized there was some sort of depth to our relationship.

Then a relative of your died, and I had no idea what to do. So, I coordinated with the flower shop to get the kind of flowers that would bring some sort of comfort. It was hard to have the words to say, because I didn't want to cross a line.

You showed me perseverance, to be strong when all possible, and to celebrate people well. When my birthday came around, you brought me to your breathtaking home, took me out to eat, and to an appointment. You gave me advice, wisdom, and always made sure to listen to my concerns. My thoughts didn't go unnoticed or feel like too much. You cared about all the details.

You had a quiet way about showing up for my milestones. You showed up to my graduation party without making a fuss, always trying to direct the spotlight on someone else, even though your husband was battling something the whole town was talking about. You cared deeply our community and did anything you could to contribute, while also being the most involved and nurturing mother/wife. You did it all, while never taking credit or wanting anything in return. You taught me a lot my last two years of high school, providing me with a thirst for life and a hunger for the hurting.

We didn't see each other for almost three years, and one day you invited me over for brunch at your new home that was best equipped for your husband's declining health. You made the most delicious quiche, making me feel like every bite was the next step to heaven.

Your husband was beyond excited to see me. He always showed kindness to me, being even more generous, gentle, humble, gracious, intellectual, and making everyone feel like they were at home in his heart. He showed me how content he was with the time he had left, he saw it as a blessing from God. You sometimes came off a little guarded, while your husband had the biggest heart, and most open personality I had ever met.

I didn't want to leave after our few hours together. I could have stayed forever in the presence of you both.

The school year of 2018/2019 I got to visit a few more times before the text that changed everything.

I came across a picture of one of your kids on social media and sent it to you, making you angry and uncomfortable. You shared that you and I were friends, but that your kids weren't a part of our relationship, and if I couldn't accept that, I needed to delete your number.

I was crushed. I wondered what was going on.

That was the last time we communicated.

While you left me hurt, I'm also left with the most humbling experiences. You impacted my life in more ways than one, showing me to be more generous.

I'll forever be in awe of your intriguing, sometimes guarded, exquisite self. My France, my love, thank you.

"Every great soul had a great mentor." —Lailah Gifty Akita.

The Teacher

I don't remember how we met, other than you were a 4th grade teacher that everyone loved. I didn't have the pleasure of having you as my own teacher, but a lot of my friends did, so I would try to visit your room to get a glimpse of this love everyone was talking about. They were right. You had a lot of love to give.

It wasn't until my junior year that I got to know you better. You saw something in yourself that you knew I needed. For a year we met a handful of times, you always asking beyond the "how are you?" question. You insisted on spoiling me the early morning of my 17th birthday before school. That was the day I knew you loved me. I felt like you showered me with it.

I'm convinced your steady example, love, devotion, and faith helped me survive junior year. You helped me become more bold in my faith that year and to this day I'm forever grateful.

You stepped out of my life for 5 years, and entered back in unexpectedly. I was content with what you did my junior year, but God had other plans.

You and I met at a coffee shop while I had another mentor obsessively on my mind. You are so good at reading people that you asked me about it. You were friends with this mentor, but not like close friends. You offered your perspective, but I was drowning in my own insecurities, so whatever you were going to share with me was never going to be good enough. I wish I would have given you more of me that day, but you relentlessly gave me grace anyway.

For the next few months you continued to show up, love me, taking me on exhilarating adventures, and praying with me. You were so kind, generous, gracious, honest, patient, and loving to me.

The last time we spent alone time together was January 4th, 2020. You asked me to go snow-shoeing with you, which was so much fun. It was also 3 days before my sister died. I honestly can't remember why you excited my life once again other than an upcoming pandemic and being busy.

In the fall of 2021 I kept getting the urge to talk to you, so one afternoon I decided to call you after not speaking for 1.5 years. You answered right away. We caught up for an hour, and I told you I was in the midst of writing my first book. You mirrored my level of excitement, which was everything to me. We talked about getting together, even me coming to visit while you would be watching your grandson.

But, then a week goes by, and you decided to send me a text telling me you don't know why you said yes to me coming over without asking your son, and that you feel we shouldn't be in each other's lives due to me being disappointed in you at times.

I was crushed. That was the last time we communicated, because after you ignored my texts. Something I didn't understand.

The way you left this time stung, because I was used to you communicating strong and firm things to my face. What I came to terms with is that it's more about the other person than it has to do about you. I couldn't take what you did so personally. You must have had something going on.

What stung turned to radical joy. I can look back and think of the joy of our last phone conversation. That's what I can hold onto. Joy, Jesus, and the walk. You're such a faithful servant of Word, wanting others to be disciplined by the Word rather than the world.

I am content by the faithfulness of your walk with Jesus and your walk on my path. I can't change your last text, but I can change the perspective I have on our relationship.

I know over time we will have coffee and another adventure whether it is with our feet on the ground or in the sky, it will be a blessing in disguise.

Part 3:
Adulthood:
every breath of hallelujah

"You have to learn how to get comfortable with being uncomfortable."
—Lou Piniella.

My Obsessive One

I thought we would be friends forever. But, here's the thing: When you get upset I would be hanging out with other friends or wanting to spend more time with other people, it made me realize I was friends with someone who was possessive. I didn't want to lose you, so I kept trying to force the friendship to stay as it was, but your heart kept hardening as time went on.

We were both 18, new students at our college, barely breathing, anticipating husbands, but settling for any friendship.

You were shy, not as outgoing, introverted, and would much rather spend time with people in an enclosed space. My heart did soften to your calm and steady way of doing things. I thank you for that.

I knew I loved you and cared so much about you. I also knew that I felt like I was being let out of cage when we would be done hanging out. I was so confused when I would miss you when you'd leave home for weekends, but also, I'd feel like I was granted visiting hours with my other friends. The feelings changed when winter came around, because I picked up on the game, the unhealthy friendship.

I remember we planned to stop through a drive-thru when I would plan to drop the bomb. It was the worst timing it felt, but there was never going to be a good time to share what I needed to tell you. I needed to end our friendship. I was already having so many issues with other people, but this friendship gave me full blown anxiety. We both had things going on separately that robbed us of, at times, growing close to our Savior. This friendship only proved of that even more. I told you that we couldn't go on like this anymore. You wouldn't look at me, shocked by my own confession and desires of how to move forward. I didn't know what to do. I thought, "do I hug her? Pray with her? Should I just get out of the car?" My thoughts ran mad, intensifying as silence was the only thing left between us. The silence was awkward and I felt so uncomfortable. I don't remember much more of that night.

But, the weeks and months were so uncomfortable. Then one day, I realized after several weeks, you stopped showing up. You left and ran home. You disappeared just like that. I blamed myself - for a short while - of your disappearance. I wondered if I made a mistake ending our friendship. God revealed to me later that what I did was brave, that I needed to give myself grace. He had something even better for me, I just had to wait.

Our friendship taught me that I needed to get comfortable being uncomfortable. Being obedient to God doesn't mean I'll always be comfortable with what He asks of me, but it'll be more than worth it.

My Gentle One

There's so much I could say about you, but I feel I could never bring justice to the way your being brought maturity and understanding to my life. In any situation that was either painful or uncomfortable, you always came in for a hug. Still, to this day, it has an impact on my way of going through conflict.

I was only a freshman and you were a senior when we met. We both worked at the library at our college, and you quickly became an older sister, mentor to me. You showed me what a good wife was, a healthy relationship between two people, and the kind of boundaries you need.

One day, after only knowing you for a month, I decided to write you a long letter of gratitude, and love. The letter came across too strong, uncomfortable, and it left you in a confused state of mind. You reached out to someone who was wise, my own RA, and wondered what to do. You could have left me, allowed things to be awkward, but you chose grace. It was awkward for me for a while, because I didn't know how I should talk to you going forward, let alone act around you. I felt as if I was walking on eggshells for quite some time, and you quickly picked up on my own discomfort. You asked me for coffee to talk about everything. I was on the edge of my seat the whole time, anxiety on high. You were so calm, confident, kept looking at me with concern, reminding me ever so often how deeply loved I was, and you were always reassuring. Soon after, you became the calm in the storm my freshman year. We became even closer after that situation, you chose to get to know my heart better, and you became aware of my situation.

You are a rare breed, my gentle one, because there were plenty of times you could have left my freshman year or given up catching up with me over the years, but your deep love, unwavering heart, and always seeking for intimacy in any connection you make with people, really profoundly moves me. Thank you for showing me all of that.

Your lessons still have a way of playing out in my life, sometimes creeping in when least expecting it, and that's a good thing. We haven't seen each other in three years, but I look forward to being reunited over a picnic with your children, embracing all the love, closeness, and laughter. I love you, endlessly, my gentle one.

My Big Curls

When we met you were a senior nursing student with a lot going on, and I was a freshman who had never been to a private Christian school (other than preschool!).

You had brown hair, with the biggest of curls that reminded me of Shirley Temple. I thought you were from a different country just by the insane amount of beauty and the difference in your way of being. I couldn't quite put it into words.

The first few times that I had seen you, you were in a rush to get somewhere, and you'd smile so big and say, "Hiya!" (That was the way you were, to greet each person as if they were your friend.) I knew I needed to get to know you, but didn't know how. I was so distracted by other friendships that it felt impossible to go and figure you out.

But, then one evening became my favorite divine intervention God had. I was sitting on the stairs, texting people back, and waiting for the next thing, when all of a sudden, I see you happily walking up the stairs. My heart did a few somersaults. I said with courage and nervousness, "Can we talk tonight?" You said, "Hold on! I'll be right back!" You quickly grabbed something from your room, and when you came back, you sat right next to me to explain that you had prior engagements, but that we could meet over the weekend. It was all in how you approached it that showed me you were different and that I was beyond thrilled to spend alone time with you.

On the day of, you changed the times, so that I could come up to your place without any distractions from people. You had messaged me a few times on Facebook messenger. I was beyond nervous. I thought, "Will I let this girl in? Could she be my friend or mentor? Will she be open with me?" I lived on the first level, while you lived on the third, so there was some walking and thinking that could be done before actually making it to your room.

You had a sweatshirt on with sweatpants while your hair was down, and you looked more beautiful than ever. We sat on your comfortable couch to talk about anything and everything, you welcomed every inch of me. That both frightened me and exhilarated me. The combination often left me breathless in between taking turns to talk, but I was more than eager to learn about you. You were the kind of friend that allowed people to lean in, give them freedom to talk about their struggles, and then give room to sit in the uncomfortable while also celebrating the person for all that they were. You had that gift.

It was so hard to leave your couch that day, because you made our time together feel so precious. What came out of the time spent together we both weren't prepared for or expecting.

Eventually you gave me your phone number, and our texting relationship often caused friction between us. Our way of communicating was different. I'd say 98% of any friction we had was over a screen, not in person. Sometimes I wonder what would have happened if we kept our friendship purely for face-to-face.

As time went on we became so close. Any chance I could get I wanted to spend time with you. You were insanely busy in your last year of being a nursing student, something I could never understand. But, I would often try to be respectful of our time together, sometimes setting 30 minute timers, so that you could go back to studying. I never had a friendship that required that, but I knew I didn't want to lose you.

People would comment on our friendship from time to time. I remember one time I came to the library after a long day, and we stood in the middle of the walkway hugging for a long time. A girl walked by saying, "this is the cutest thing I've ever seen. Friendship goals." I thought we were. I also thought you gave the purest form of hugs. I could have stood in your presence all night, because your light was everything.

When Christmas break came around the corner, I still couldn't believe I was your friend. You meant the world to me, and my gosh, I was going to make sure you knew it. I didn't have much money, but I saved some up to get you a personalized gift. I gave you a keychain that symbolized faith with your name on it, and a message on the back letting you know you'd make an amazing nurse someday. You were so happy, like any other time I'd written a long letter, which I tried to do a lot.

Coming back from break I was ashamed by the mistakes I made, and knew there were amends that I needed to make. I'll never forget the first day I got back and deciding to bring my little brother up to meet you. You came up to me right away to hug me so tight. Again, I felt unworthy, but you showed me God's character once again.

I decided to take you out to Olive Garden to extend an apology and try to make things right. We talked for 3 hours that night, much longer than we've talked alone before.

Over the next several months I carried with me all the mistakes I made in our friendship the first semester. I was dragging myself into a pit of sadness. I allowed the enemy in too many times. I should have just let go and allowed God to do His work. Would that have been too hard? I don't know.

Here's what you taught me: nobody can be my Savior, only God can. That if God has called me to it, He will walk me through it. And, you showed me how to try to love people like Jesus does.

I haven't seen you since 2018, but here's the thing: I so badly wanted to be your friend, for you to love me, for you to see me, understand me, to see that I was worthy enough, and that I was also so broken. The thing is you tried, you grew tired of everything. I also wasn't letting you see everything.

When I dream of our reunion I see us sitting across the table from one another, and you beaming with delight over the goodness and favor God has brought to my life. That I actually grew, matured even.

I sing hallelujah now and amen for the faithfulness and grace you brought to my life, and I'll praise God for His divine intervention when we see each other again. Until I'm in your presence again, I'll dance to the rare love you lavished over my life.

My Forbidden Flower

Out of all the friendships I've ever had, I wonder how I stumbled on your kingdom.

When we first met, I still had some walls up, but in a lot of ways you reminded me of my 5th grade best friend, and I was keen on bringing back that child-like wonder. It took all of our freshmen year of college of being in a few classes together, even receiving help from you in one class, volunteering at the same church on Wednesdays to even contemplate the idea of being friends. I didn't know your reasoning for the holdup, but I knew mine. Somehow our hearts softened and the idea of grabbing coffee didn't feel like a horrible idea.

In the middle of June, on a beautiful warm day, we met up at a cute coffee shop where I let some of my walls down, but not all the way, and you gave me the chance to go on about life. Somewhere in between our conversation I thought to myself, "My gosh I'm having so much fun. Is she, too?" I tried to soak in everything you were saying, trying to show you that I cared so much of what you had to say. I wanted you to know that I was so grateful you were there with me and that I was willing to learn from you.

We ended our hang out by watching the movie Heaven is for Real at your welcoming and joyful home. I was taken back by how wonderful of a time I had, because I haven't experienced an amazing hang out with someone in a long while, and I wondered, "Is she just another friend that will only last a year?"

I threw up my hands, full of anticipation that she would run, but she pursued me more and more as the months went on. She saw something lovely and complicated in me and decided I was worthy enough. What I saw in her was a girl that was full of light, compassion, joy, and gentleness. As time went on for me, I saw, too, that she was lovely and complicated, but I thought, "Even if things don't work out, how amazing I got to bear witness to this kind of light."

After that initial first coffee, the summer came and went. I had another opportunity to meet with you before school started and I wasn't going to mess that up. You ended up moving to our college a few weeks early due to being on the leadership team and said that I could come hang with you for a bit. When I drove to the campus that evening I didn't know what would happen.

I got out of my car with excitement worn all over my face. I needed to see you. As I got closer to the door, I could see you sitting down with other girls on the couch watching something. I felt like I was interrupting something, but I kept up with my own pace and gravitated towards the stairs. I knocked on the door, and you instantly turned your head with a smile. I wondered, "Is she as excited to see me as I am to see her?" You came in with a hug smelling like fruits. That was the last hug we would experience as just friends, for we were moving to territories of deepening a friendship that neither of us planned for.

We tried to focus on whatever we were watching, but kept finding ways back to conversation. We talked a lot until we realized how late it was and the longevity of my drive back. It was hard to find the courage to get up and leave, but we both had busy weeks ahead of us. We both had to prepare in different ways for our sophomore year of college.

I don't think we realized until the first day back to school how many classes we had together. I only had four classes, but you were in three of them. It was the start of a very complicated, confusing, joyful, and amazing journey.

I think it was a compilation of having so many classes together, being in the same program, and living so close together that helped build our relationship. Almost everyday during the school week we would grab coffee or a snack in the coffee shop inside of our school. We would also study long hours in the library together as well.

Every bit of the way you showed me God's grace and forgiveness. Something that was lost a lot in previous relationships. That's what made me gravitate to you more, and what made me push you away.

As the seasons began to change and signs of fall were evident, our friendship deepened. Like I said I believe it was the time spent, but one night just wasn't like the other. Our hugs changed, too, by the result of this single night.

On the last day of September, we spent all day in class, then grabbed coffee, and talked for a few hours. We took pictures and then went to our separate dorms. The hangout was nothing special or exciting. It's interesting how you can go from a regular hang out with a friend to meeting in the living room late at night. Everything shifted, changed, and became ever so real. We talked about our future, surface level things, then I asked the one deep question that changed the way of friendships for me. I asked, "So what do you struggle with?"

The question seems so simple now, but at 19 years old asking that involved a lot of courage, sacrifice, and the willingness to be so vulnerable. I wasn't too keen on being vulnerable, but there you were with an open heart ready to kick what the enemy deemed wrong. The enemy didn't want us to take the risk or get close.

You opened up, while looking deeply in my eyes, with nervousness, unsure if I could handle the information. I gasped, because I, too, struggled the same way. We each took turns sharing piece by piece, because it was all new and scary sharing something so intimate and private. We talked until two in the morning. You were so accepting of me, which was too good to believe. It was hard for both of us to stop talking and return to our rooms. But, I could see your eyes grow heavy with wonder still sparkling.

That night was everything to me. You found out the deepest and darkest secret about me, and you are still the only one who knows. What we shared was a touch of heaven, I'm convinced.

As time went on we had carved out something for the both of us once a week. In the midst of trying, there were disagreements, moments you thought I was too much. From October to December we were tested with everything and we even one time had a mentor mediate our conversation. As much as the enemy tried to destroy our friendship we kept getting closer. We both would look at each other saying, "I don't think we could get closer if we tried." But, we did. We would surprise each other. We found ways to spend more time together, even if our other friends joined. We never went a day without texting each other. Saying, "I love you," was always said.

You kept showing me the means of compassion. You showed me how to grow towards Christ, and how to find a way to break my heart for things that Jesus' heart broke for.

The real test for our friendship was Christmas break. I said some stuff that didn't make sense to you, things that made you uncomfortable even. It should have been the end of our friendship, but as the weeks went on you exemplified grace, love, and forgiveness. We were able to spend time together once during our break and that was so lovely to the both of us.

Once we got back everything changed. You changed. I changed. It wasn't the first day back to campus, but it happened rapidly. Tensions were high, drama felt unavoidable, and I grew in sickness. We still found ways to deepen our relationship and everything was or seemed okay until it wasn't. Six weeks in I found out again that you were talking about me behind my back. It should have been a warning sign the first time, but I was sucked into your world, mesmerized by your beauty and grace. I thought, "How could the one person I trust with everything be continuously talking about me?" I couldn't believe it. Rumors started, too. I felt like I couldn't breathe. All I wanted was for you and I to just figure it out. I still wanted you and I knew you wanted me, too.

After all the turmoil, we decided on a break after praying together, which turned into a permanent one. When the break started I began a painful, unthinkable, life-altering journey of healing. For the next 6 weeks I bawled everyday. I wasn't awake, I needed a revelation. I needed to surrender fully, to be completely vulnerable with God and well, with myself, too. I'd sing to myself, "Jesus I will trust you. I know you'll never fail me. I know you're in the unknown." I kept trying to have the faith that you and I would find our way back to each other. What I should have been praying for was God to reveal to me why the relationship wasn't worth running back to.

Jesus never failed. He provided the utmost healing while I was dealing with the terrible sadness. He used so many people to speak truth to me, drown me with love, and suffocate me with hugs. I really thought that it was going to be impossible to get over the hurt of our friendship. But, you weren't there and that hurt, but God was. He kept showing His faithfulness, gentleness, never-ending love, purpose, and provision.

We haven't talked for a few years now, but I have a lot to be grateful for. You taught me what I needed in a friendship. I believe it is because of our friendship that I was able to learn the warning signs.

You are beautiful and there are days I wish I could pick up the phone to tell you what I've been up to. I think you'd be proud, shocked even by the transformation and growth done. But, this I know: I love you, my forbidden flower.

My Forbidden Fruit

If you were coffee, I'd want to lick off the carmel whip cream, and savor every sip. If you were chocolate, I'd let the melting points sit on my taste buds. Hm. Sometimes you felt like the forbidden fruit in the garden of eden. The fruit might seem sweet and savory, but really poison.

I feel our friendship started as two young deer galloping in the field, young, pure, and free. At the time, you were a mom of two and newly married. I was 20 years old, a junior in college, and living with a relative.

Our bond and connection took a while to pick up speed. But, once it did, hours became minutes. We would hang out 1-2 times a month, talk once a day for about four months. When December came around, I noticed something crumble inside my heart. I wondered if you were going to run like forbidden flower had 6 months prior. My heart was still so fragile, broken, and not ready to step into another deep friendship, but at the same time, I was craving someone to see me, hear me, to love me. I know it's not good that you were a rebound friend for me.

When we planned for a Christmas gathering, I was beyond excited and also, extremely nervous. At this point of our friendship, whenever we would get together, my heart would do a few somersaults. For some reason whenever I get closer to people, I become more nervous to be around them, often leading to getting cotton mouth. So, showing up to your house on that cold December day felt like I was just given the task of giving a speech to millions of people.

We had fun that day, and that was also the day you saw right through my changed demeanor, which was terrifying and freeing. You said, "Are you okay? Your whole demeanor changed." I remember my heart sinking, feeling ever particle take a vacation down my body. I watched as my body was unleashing the uncomfortable, the incredibly intimate feeling, and then my body did a cold shake as if to wake myself up.

You still might be the only friend that has been able to read me that well.

As time went on, I saw signs that our friendship was unhealthy due to the rift that would happen with constantly snap-chatting each other. We would argue more and more, never really working out anything in person. Things would go under the rug, something that I was taught to never do, but as with any friendship I had, I was just grateful to have a friend.

Our friendship brought out the impulsive side in me as in renting a limo on my 21st birthday with only making $10.40/hr at my job. It might have been fun spending a few hours in a limo with you, feeling the extravagant and glamorous life for a second, but looking back, I should have just went out to breakfast with you.

When summer came around, our friendship became obsessive, and I stopped seeing my own friends regularly. I only wanted to see you, spend time with you. This led me to getting another expensive gift for you. A bracelet with your name engraved into it with a special message on the inside of the bracelet. The gift was absolutely beautiful and precious, but no matter how hard I tried to salvage our friendship, things become more toxic and unhealthy. I was so attached at this point, somehow blind to the consequences of the summer months. Every time I tried to work out a miscommunication, you'd tell me we couldn't talk on the phone or that you felt in your spirit that it wouldn't be right to meet in person.

On October 18, 2018 was the end of our snapchat relationship, and the beginning of our longest break we had ever taken in our friendship. You said we were done, something I was expecting several months prior, but I just remember feeling weird. I was expecting to feel intense amount of sadness, pain, but all I felt was numb, and this was a first for me after a friendship breakup. The numbness stayed on high frequency while I had reunions with people I had not seen in months or years. When the numbness subsided, sadness creeped in, and I didn't even try to shove the feeling away. I invited the feeling for all its glory and agony, often wondering where the past year of my life had went. The sadness turned to anger, and I was angry for 3 months, when all of sudden, you unexpectedly reached out to me to tell me you had my book. I was trying to move on with my life, and your message distracted my vision. After the messaging stopped, the anger continued on for a few more weeks, and then I reached acceptance. I needed to accept that our friendship was unhealthy and toxic, that the amount of messages we would send in a day was way too much.

Over time we would catch up a few times a year, often over messages never over the phone or in person. We've seen each other twice at an event and a funeral since the fallout of our friendship in 2018. When the only option was to use social media to connect, and you didn't want to have in person conversations, I had to walk away (in the fall of 2021) knowing the most healthy thing is for us to not be following each other on social media. Sometimes the most loving thing you can do is put space and distance between two hearts, knowing the relationship only causes rift and destruction.

There are beautiful pieces of art you've left on my heart. The gift of spending time with your children, learning more about discernment from the Bible and seeking the Spirit at all times, and to seek justice in every stigma thrown my way.

We got the closure we needed, most do not get that, and for that, I'm at peace, and grateful for the work of God. To winning for the Kingdom always and forever, my forbidden fruit.

My Unexpected

When I got to touch your presence, that's when I knew there was a depth about you, some anxiety to you, and I knew I needed to be a part of that. For some reason I was intrigued about your insecurities, your issues, because you painted the perfect, silly life on social media and I was convinced there was something more about you.

I don't know what it is about mom's, but I'm drawn to their perfume, and you had your own. I had the rare opportunity of obtaining a relationship with almost all of your kids. Being in soccer with your oldest daughter, graduating with your son, becoming friends with your other daughter, and being a friendly face for your youngest daughter at events. You've watched me grow up through the relationships I've had with your children, often highlighting my not-so-good moments.

When the fallout of my friendship happened with your daughter and I, I thought that would be the end of getting to know you better. I was ashamed, feeling like I would lose a beautiful mama I could turn to. But, as time went on, you showed grace and humor in my unlikely favor. You even sent me a lovely card for my high school graduation. As I grew older and as we had more messages sent between us, my heart grew tender and relaxed towards you.

In 2018, something in my heart knew I needed to see you, and if by chance tell you what I had been holding on to for years. One day I messaged you asking if you'd be in the building of one of your businesses. You completely rocked my world by saying, "When you're town, message me! It would be great to see you! Maybe we could even meet at Ellie's!" My heart did a thousand somersaults. I thought, "wow! This woman who has been an inspiration for years wants to meet up with me alone?!" It all worked out, due to God's divine timing, because we were able to not only meet at an ice cream shop, but also one of the businesses you own. It was two hours of bliss, slowly letting my walls come down, and leaning into any kind of wisdom you might bestow upon me. When it came down to finally sharing what I had been holding on to, I was beyond nervous, and you looked curious while also wearing nervousness on your fingertips. It was different for me to see you in this kind of state of mind, but I knew I needed to be courageous. Each word, each breath felt like freedom, watching the enemy lose its power, and watching you lead me to the presence of healing. You said, "oh honey. You can let that go. We never held that over you." I felt so loved by you at that moment.

Over the next few months you accepted becoming my mentor for my senior year of college, a decision you didn't take lightly. Things were great, until trying to get together felt impossible and I kept coming back to feelings of pity. I didn't want you to mentor me because you felt you had a moral responsibility or that you felt bad for me, I wanted you to because you felt it as an honor to help me grow. This led to the first rift in which you tried to calm me down, letting me know life has just been crazy and you didn't pity me.

But, as sweet as you were, as generous had you been, and wisdom-filled, I couldn't shake the feelings. I read into every single text you sent after, driving me to utter craziness.

One day I told you, while on vacation, to block me without any context. In my defense, you told me you had been meaning to message me for a while, because you felt you were letting me down, and that I would get upset with you. That you didn't know to even think about going forward due to the decision I had already made in my head. That was the end of the mentorship. I was so heartbroken, knowing the way things ended should not have occurred. But, you still wished me well over text message on my graduation day, something that was planned by our amazing God.

Your character always left me surprised. You are firm & polite, but warm & giving mixed in with some anxiety. The combo took me years to understand.

You always reminded me that I had a special gift to give to the world, that you sincerely wanted the best for me always.

In our reunion, I hope I'm treating you to ice-cream talking about all of the silliness that life has to offer, and gosh that image makes me giddy. I love you, my unexpected gift.

My Savior

What was selfish was that I kept trying to put unrealistic expectations on you. I kept seeing Jesus in you, that you had a perfection about you, but you were broken like me just trying to live each day for Christ.

It's crazy, because you have five beautiful kids, and the fact that I got to witness a few months of your sweetness should leave me grateful, but I think it's how you left is what makes me bitter at times. I can't help, but look back on every single thing I said to you, the way I acted around you. There have been times I've obsessed over every little thing that happened between us, the game driving me to madness.

Our story begins with me witnessing a powerful testimony over video that led me to my knees, but ultimately gave me courage to reach out to you. I made the brave act, because I saw something beautiful from the start and I wanted to see what God could do. I didn't think the brave act would lead you to asking me to meet for coffee. I just wanted a few messages between you and I, because you were interesting to me and I wanted to know a bit more, but I thought it would be nearly impossible to get together due to your position. But, you were curious about me, you wanted to help, and so you asked about my living situation, schedule, etc.

It was June of 2019 and I was freshly 22 years old, just had graduated with my bachelors. I was filled with anxiety and anticipation, hungry for what Jesus might do.

I showed up at the coffee shop 15 minutes early afraid that I might be late. You showed up right on the dot with your baby in a stroller. You smiled so big like we had been friends forever and I instantly felt 60% of my anxiety subside.

I had never met with someone privately who had a lot of influence on people as in over 100,000 people. But, out of sheer obedience, you decided to take 90 minutes out of your day to meet with me.

You bought me coffee, and then we went for a long walk. I remember being so lost in the beauty and calmness in how you approached your words. You created a safe place for me to open up about my own pain of having an inconsistent dad, something we both could relate on. Although, your dad, eventually after many years, decided to give up the half life, and commit to being an amazing dad in your later adulthood. You didn't try to diminish the pain I felt about my dad, but instead validated every feeling I had about him and our story.

You ended our time together with prayer that left me speechless. I'm so grateful for that time spent together on that day.

For the next two months we kept in contact over Facebook messenger, something that was easy for me.

One time when I had bad news I wondered if I should call you, because you have five kids and a husband, and so many other things. You allowed me to call you while you were nursing your own child, again listening to all of my feelings, and then praying with me. You texted me after that conversation saying, "I'm sorry things didn't work out. Fall into bed and sleep well. Love you!" It was the love that brought the pain to rest, so I could actually sleep that night.

Then I wanted to get together again, only this time at our church. I kept going back and forth between committing with the idea, because I didn't want to be a burden in your life. I often felt that with others.

When we met for church with you and your kids, I felt like we were in the zoo. Everyone wanted your attention and love. I didn't understand what it was like to be a pastors wife, the pressure it had to be on you, but I also didn't try my best to understand either.

We had brief conversations and at one point someone came up to you, and you introduce me saying, "I'm Krystalann's mentor." To which both surprised me and took me back. I thought, "Was she really mentoring me?"

The last time I saw you when things were still okay was August 2019. You actually sent me a message 45 minutes before I was going to walk into church. You said, "I wish I could give you everything you need, but I know God gives us exactly what we need in every season." You added a bunch of kiss emojis. The message confused me, because did that mean, "the end of our mentoring??" I wasn't ready. I thought, "do I still walk into church now with these big emotions?" I decided that I should anyway, because I was already in the parking lot. When I got to the doors, I was still so shocked by my pain and confusion. But, just as I went to find a seat, I found you sitting, holding your baby. I didn't know what to say, but I decided to sit by you, and you, with some walls up, allowed me to sit by you. It was so strange. You felt like the amazing lady I knew, yet your body language was telling me something different. I tried to ignore it, but as the service went on, I could feel the uneasiness. I got to spend time with your kids a bit after church, but then you guys all left.

That night I went to Facebook messenger to find out I was no longer able to send you a message. I was crushed. I thought, "what could I have possibly done??"

The next day I contacted a pastor to explain what happened, to which the praying pastor was surprised by what I was sharing with him. He said, "could it be that she deactivated her account?" Perhaps. But, I couldn't help, and wondered, "why would she deactivate and not say anything about being done mentoring or something?" It felt bizarre.

I tried to continue on with my life, but my heart was crushed. I felt like another mentor gave up on me.

. . .

The next time I saw you was December 2019. I saw you in a row of people, but thought I should tap you and say hi. You were shocked and cold. I again questioned myself.

The last time I saw you was January 2021. I saw you from a distance at church. My mom and I were talking with people, and my eyes kept finding ways to look at you. I felt guilty, sad, and still overwhelmed with emotions.

Your kids found ways to stare at me, and I felt like they just knew. I was crippled by guilt.

Even though it's been three years since you were actively in my life, I still think of you ever so often, wondering how you might be.

I thank God for the times that we shared, convinced that the wisdom you shared with me still helps me to this day. So, for that I'm grateful. That doesn't mean I don't think about that last summer day.

*"I looked in the mirror, not shocked at the tear stains on my shirt,
not even sure what I looked like anymore without swollen eyes.
This was the moment I realized sad had become the ordinary and
all else was merely the exception."* —Bella Mayo

My Coffee

Your absence showed me that my presence never mattered to you. It showed me that even the most loved person in a small town can quickly flip the light switch. You showed me how.

You'd always remind me to channel my anger to something I love and in that to bring joy. You would always remind me to seek joy in everyday life, in the small things and the big things. That life is such a gift, that I'm one and so was our relationship.

Our relationship began with trying to build it on a firm foundation of love, faith, devotion, early mornings, and peaceful summer days. Our relationship, when I reflect back on it, reminds me of the essence of summer, the beauty, the grace, the tranquility, the never-ending fun.

You were the healer that brought writing back into my life. Our times together reflected that and it's led a lot of people to believing the good about God.

You were the hot cup of coffee in the morning, the cooling lemonade in the afternoon, and the hot coco in the evening. A lot of people would agree and I love that.

You have the power to bring a smile to my face and lose sleep over excitement to see you. Yet, you have no power of making me feel like I am not worthy to be forgiven or given grace.

My soul rests in knowing that one day you'll see and that you'll feel the Holy Spirit's convictions. You are sweet & joyful, and I'd love nothing more than to be greeted by one of your genuine hugs, but we can't go back and play games now.

I love you and always will, my coffee & lover of summer.

"Butterflies can't see their wings. They can't see how truly beautiful they are, but everyone else can. People are like that as well." — Naya Rivera.

My Sensitive One

Isn't it just like heaven when you hold me close to your chest? You remind me a lot of the person from My Coffee, except with a lot more depth and sensitivity. You're wise, gentle, sensitive, and crave intimate connection much like me. Our time together has always reflected in that and maybe even a touch of heaven.

The last time we saw other was December 2021. I can remember the morning so vividly, the feeling in my heart, how my stomach was reacting, and how my body was moving. I was excited, but nervous. Nervous, because our time together usually mean going to uncharted territories, allowing the Holy Spirit to use you to go the unholy parts of my heart, and trusting I'll be okay when we are finished. It's scary, it's intimate, and it's healing.

But, it's so good for me. I think the hard thing about our relationship was: the messaging and the fact you thought I came on too strong at times. A phrase that comes as a trigger to me. I wish it wasn't, and I wish it wasn't the very thing that allowed the enemy to take a foothold in our relationship.

You've taught me to stay a little longer rather than rushing out when things are uncomfortable. I've experienced more than enough uncomfortable moments with you and wanting to run, but watching fire ignited when our hearts stayed in the room was always the glimpse of heaven I needed.

Your voice of reason still shows up when I'm discerning or experiencing the scary depths of relationships.

I heard that when we force someone to stay in our life longer than they are meant to be, God hardens their heart, because there's no other reason to be ghosted by you. So as much as I want to say, "come a little closer, stay a little longer", I can rest in knowing that your teachings, your love, our therapeutic meetings are something I can carry with me forever. And, I can be grateful for any student who stumbles on your path, because I know they will get a touch of heaven, and their own breath into hallelujah.

My Home

"Hi! Can you pray for my brother?" You said, "Sure! What's his name?"

That's the first time I remember a conversation with you and it was fall of 2019, while helping my mom clean the church. It was the start of something both of us didn't see coming, but God planted a seed that day.

It wasn't until a whole entire year later, when my brother was sent to treatment for the first time, that we corresponded, and you and your husband encouraged my mom and I. I saw that the living word of God was all over you and your husband's heart.

As time went on, I saw the Lord's favor and faithfulness. I saw you open the door to your home for the first time, and I saw my heart fall in love with your kids. It was all too easy, except ironically the bond between you and I didn't really take off until the summer of 2021. It took a little bit to see the depth in your heart. Once we moved to a stronger and deeper relationship, I found myself receiving more check-in texts from you, more hugs, more phone conversations, and more love. You moved to a role of being a second mother, the kind that encouraged me the most. I was on my knees a lot due to the unexpected blessing you had over my life.

When things got real too quick in December of 2021, I wanted to walk away. It seemed like the best possible outcome, only leaving you confused and feeling defeated. I needed the Lord to do the work on my heart.

You were never far, which at times, in my own anger made me want to lash out at you. Eventually, silence was the only thing we had left between us.

That was when God moved into my heart, shifted it on things high above. Slowly, by summer 2022, our hearts, tender & careful, found themselves together again. I was able to walk right into your house like we didn't have something happen between us, and that's when I knew something was far different with your family than any I had ever spent time with. The whole family greeted me and looked at me with so much love.

You've taught me a lot. You set an example of a giving, nurturing, and selfless mother.

You made your house the home of my heart, and I can't wait to see where the Lord blesses us next. You are the home I never saw coming, but the home I needed to see to get proof of good Christians and the faithfulness of a community. Thank you for showing me that you could see past my ugly, and instead invite room for growth & grace. What the enemy tried to destroy between us, God gave us armor to defeat, and we can now rejoice, because the war is over. I love you, my home.

"To be a Christian means to forgive the inexcusable because God has forgiven the inexcusable in you." —C.S. Lewis.

My Awakening

When we first met you asked me what sign I was. Not what my name was or how I was, but my sign. I thought, "here we go again with someone wanting to assume who I am based on when I was born." Yet, I was captivated by your curiosity, your boldness, and your somewhat nervousness. You had such a determined and forceful, yet gentle way of your coming toward me.

After two weeks of spending 8 hour work days together and allowing some walls to fall, we decided to get together, only for my own heart to freak out. I was convinced you didn't want to really get together. I texted you saying, "never mind." I remember instantly regretting it, because I wanted to see you and spend time with you.

So, with planting the seed once again another few weeks later, I asked you if we could get together. You smiled effortlessly, and said, "when?!"

When we decided on a day, I had one issue with myself. "Was I going to let my walls come completely down?" I decided to do the wait-and-see approach.

I can't forget the nervousness I was feeling all day and how long the hours felt. I couldn't wait to finally spend time with you alone. We've had so much distraction coming up to this moment.

I'll never forget the minutes before. I felt like a kid witnessing a candy store for the first time. I knew it was going to be sweet, but didn't know how sweet.

You opened the door quickly with a half smile and appearing as if you had something mulling over on your mind. I wondered what you wanted to say, but all you said was, "I forgot what I was going to do." I couldn't help, but laugh.

We spent the next four hours watching a show that you resonated so deeply with. The show was unexpecting, disturbing, wild, exciting, and yet, uncomfortable. I felt not ready to be soaked into that world when I was already experiencing bits of that world at home. It was painful, too, and it brought up some emotions. The emotions led me to turn to face to your beautiful face. It was then that I decided to let everything go. I told you some things of my past, watching myself grow more emotional with every detail, and then catching glimpses of sadness wash across your face. You listened so intently, asking questions when it was appropriate, and you tried to hold back the tears. The room shifted, as if the director did a panorama of the conversation. You looked at me as I continued on, and then the tears you tried to hold back made their way down your sweet cheeks. You laid there, paralyzed by your own intense emotions. I had to find my way over to you somehow without making anything awkward. I only needed three seconds, so I decided to take it. I inched my way over to you, and you didn't hold back. You allowed me in your pain, and let me comfort you for seconds. I thought that was the moment that changed our friendship. I thought to myself, "I will finally have a good Christian friend in my life once again and she works with me, too!"

But, as I left I felt something in me that I tried to ignore. A sudden shift, perhaps a reminder from God that He had something better for me.

The next few days you changed and didn't want to talk as much. I called you out on your actions, and it was then that you threw in the towel. You were done with me, blocking me on everything.

The next five months were painful, jarring, and eye-opening. It grew into some numbing at times, because I got too attached fast and I didn't know how to handle these feelings.

I wanted you to know that I still cared and loved you, that I wanted the best for you, but space was all I could give you.

Unexpectedly, you showed up, and started making small conversation. I felt like I was in a dream, so with each small conversation I didn't take the time to process it. It had been 5 months since we last spoke, and then there you were. Eventually we talked more and more, leading to some laughing, too. After a few months of reconnecting, you told me why you had stopped talking to me and it was something that I had not even done. It shocked me, but we started talking less and less after. Another ache I wasn't expecting to happen.

But, I hope to see you again in a coffee shop, praying, where our hearts can connect, even for a minute.

My Different Religion

I'm open to learning about different cultures and religions, it's fascinating, intriguing even to find out where someone came from. It was like a huge wave slapped me across the face when I first worked with a Muslim. I thought I knew something, and I really knew nothing at all. I learned a greater capacity for love, new food, music as well as traditions.

It wasn't until 2022 that I grew immensely close to one in the community, and then more, because we are all similar, people that is. We all want the chance to be seen, heard, loved, to be valued, and yes, to be touched. The gift of touch, to be touched, to watch and feel electricity when hands come together. Some cultures, it feels, are more touchy than others, and by rare chance, I'd have the opportunity to experience the touchiest of them all.

You were so unexpected for me, often coming off as shy and not having much to say at all with a sharp edge sword. When we had the opportunity to sit down with two other gals in a circle, I'd see you often covering up your face when you'd laugh. Your face would shimmer, eyes soft and a bit dark, a smile that spoke volumes, and hands that were soft & gentle, somehow always finding your friends legs. You and your friends at this connection, being Muslim, and I was the outcast, being Christian, but it felt as if I was under this intriguing spell. I was intrigued by the way you guys spoke to one another.

As time went on, your loud and extroverted friends couldn't make the beat for me. The mysterious ones are the ones that you want to peel back layer by layer. I wanted to know your hurts, the gospel of your heart, the joys and sorrows, all of it, really. It took a while to watch your walls come down. Even then, you had so little to say, but the things left unsaid were often loud by the way your shoulders shifted.

One day I trusted you with the words in my book, I let them soak in that intelligent brain of yours. I watched as light bulbs came on, you yearning for more answers, and feeling unable to react to my tragedies. I was finally able to see another side of you, the sensitive, compassionate, and ever so curious side.

I feared to make you uncomfortable by hugging you, but as time continued on and you got further into my book, there was warmth that shed from you, and it was then that I felt it was okay to let a single finger touch you.

I wanted you to come closer, your presence was a heated blanket to my bones.

A few more times, and I found my head on your shoulders, wondering how I may have landed there. I was glued there, it was going to take me having a certain responsibility for me to get up. You held me close, allowing whatever intoxicating chemical you had in you to release onto me.

Then on a week where everything possible could go wrong and I felt my depression take over the entirety of my body, you kept checking on me. Even going out of your way to look for me, finding your way down to my level, and saying, "I was so worried about you." You had a black hijab with gold earrings on, and your face was glowing.

But, as life goes, there's ugly in everyone. You kept stringing me along, saying we would hang out, and excuses were made. A game that was played entirely too long. I was beyond done with it. The end leading you to block me, which stung and, well, it also made sense.

The quiet one who became the outspoken one. You left me breathless. You also left me confused. I don't know if we will ever be friends again or I guess attempt at a real one, but I know you had the magic wand for a lot of things.

My Butterfly

You come in with your unmatched beauty, and you greet me with dropping a bomb of love, a tide that pulls me closer to your presence. Everyone gravitates to your presence, your pull.

It's November 17th now, and that dream looks nothing like it does now. I just want to go back to November 5th, 2022. Something was entirely different about you, from anything I had ever experienced or perhaps dreamed up.

On this day, in particular, you had the most painful migraine, and I knew I was not a healer, but I had my hands. And, you, well, you had your medication and a place to lay down. I asked gently, patiently, and ever so cautiously if I could relive some of the pain. From experience I had seen from the eyes of others the work my hands could do for them, so I thought I could offer a glimpse of heaven. When my hands found your temple and increased in circular motion, the music began to change. My heart began to soften, my musicals relaxed, and I mustered up all the love in my palms. I watched as connection and healing washed over you. I watched as the pain broke through the walls of your skin, galloping out of the room, and I watched myself whisper "goodbye" to the migraine. It was as if there were several angels in the room helping me with each pressure point, making sure I made every beat and whistle, never missing the anthem. The spirit guided me, awakened & healed me. In the finale, you kept saying, "thank you" pulling me close, holding me longer than you ever have, and giving me the time to just soak up your warmth.

You never hinted that I needed to leave that cozy place, that place of security. At one point in the embrace I was worried I was staying too long, afraid I was making you uncomfortable, but as I stood up, you pulled me close once again, and I was jolted to praise. I felt as if I was on the beach sunbathing, soaking up all the vitamin D. It was perfect.

Before we left, you invited prayer to be lavished over you, and the intimacy was achieved. The touching was healing instead of triggering. Staying in the embrace was safe instead of violating. It was beautiful & free instead of sexualized & damaging.

The inner child in me needed to be nurtured, to be reminded that someone could love my damaged brain.

It reminded me again how God created us to be touched, to be seen, to be intimate with one another, and to be deeply loved. He created it for a reason. And, He, being the perfect Father, gave me a mama in that moment to take care of and to be taken care of. That's the touch of heaven He gave me.

People talk about vibes and energies these days, something I rarely bring up in conversations. That being said, your very presence pulls people to you. You are the only one I've met who has the ability to leave lingering effects. A strong connection could still be pulsating my veins two days later, making my whole body shake. I can't even explain it without still getting goosebumps. I think the Lord using you is the powerful force behind it all and I'm just grateful I could experience the magic a few times. I'm grateful for the sunshine on your palms, the rich chocolate of your hugs, and the undying comfort of your voice.

You've found your forever garden, your exact flower to be planted under the sun with. And, I've got part of your wing, all of your love stored up in a box, and when I'm ready I will dust off the shelves.

I've been praying for you, your children and your marriage. I've been hoping for you, hoping for divine intervention, to end whatever silence this is. Whatever the outcome, the Lord was such a perfect Father in orchestrating our meeting.

In your arms I find peace & safety. For now, when I put myself to sleep, I'll meet you in the clouds where dreams have no limits. You're just like heaven and our season tasted like honey. I love you.

"Let him kiss me with the kisses of his mouth - for your love is more delightful than wine." —Song of Songs 1:2.

My House of Miracles

My perfect parent, thank you for the beautiful, complicated female relationships, taking them out when it was time. You always know when to and always will.

I'm tasting honey when I think about you being the house of miracles. Even though all of these relationships didn't work out as I had hoped, I can say that I got to experience different parts of heaven, and for that, I'm eternally grateful. Each woman, so imperfectly unique, was handpicked by you, my house of miracles, to play a different role, to teach me something, and to give me even better lenses.

Your presence is my portion, your spirit can provide complete transformation and healing. Your very name has power, and you're the only perfect friend I can depend on to fulfill every void I might have. Praise be it's you.

Holy. You are holy, you're such a perfect Savior. I'll worship you forever.

Thank you for revealing the unholiness in me out of love and care for me. Thank you for being the reason I could get over the damage of being abused by women.

I love that I'm your masterpiece, that you formed in my mother's womb, knowing I'd be a woman one day, and that I could use my voice to help other women.

My favorite miracle is when you intervened, gave me courage to finally tell a woman my story, reminding me that I was worthy enough. I live for your miracles, to get my own touch of heaven.

I love that I don't have to run to my dreams to find you or to be with you. But, my favorite reunion will be just as described: white dress, in a field, with all the flowers, sun shining on my freckles, and violin playing in the background. I'll dance with you forever, hand in hand, while I'm here on earth, and then meet you at the white gates when I'm with you for eternity. Home is where You are. Jesus.